November Reflection 2020

Jan Oskar Hansen

The Author

Jan Oskar Hansen is a poet, story teller and seafarer, born in Stavanger, Norway. He joined the merchant navy at 15 and spent most of his life at sea until settling in the early 90's in Portugal. His poetry has been widely published in hard copy and online, worldwide. Reviewers have generally commented that a love and honoring of living things stands out in Hansen's work, and deep humility; that it reveals with unflinching honesty man's shortcomings in his efforts to love, telling what there is to tell in a first person, deeply resident universal voice.

The poet is widely read and fluent in several languages, knowledge often acquired at night during his many years at sea. He chose to write primarily in English following enthusiastic reception of his work from English-speaking editors and readers.

His poems have been published in over 20 literary magazines worldwide, including:

Hudson Review, USA, Skyline, USA, Skald, Wales, La rue Bella, England, The Bards, England, War is a dangerous place, England, The Black Mountain Review, Ireland, ARS Poetica India, India, Metvere Muse, India, Poets International, India, Braquemard, England, Fvirefly Magazine, USA, Pphoo, India, Taj Mahal Review, India, Remark Magazine, USA, Journal Of Anglo-Scandianvian Poetry, England.

His poems appear in the following anthologies:

Shaken & Stirred (Bewrite Books, UK, 2003), Routes – Twelve Poets (Bewrite Books, UK, 2004), A Road Less Traveled (Bewrite Books, UK, 2005), Poetry from the Far Corners (Bewrite Books, UK, 2005), Listening to the birth of crystal (Paulapublishing, 2004) England, Peoplespoet 2 (Paulapublishing, 2005) England, The Review of contemporary poetry (Bluechrome, 2005) England, The book of hopes and dreams (Bluechrome, 2006) England.

Collections "Letters from Portugal" (bewrite books) Bristol, "La Strada" (Lapwing publishers) Belfast, "End of Voyage" (WFP. New York), "Marilyn Monroe remembered" Erbacce Press. Liverpool, "The Fairground" Ranchi India (out of print now).

Contents

living in a small village

one has to deal with gossip
the trick is being polite
but not get involved.
Be friendly but not overly so.
They all have dogs,
get the animals to like you
and your neighbours will think
you are a friendly person.
Most of the villagers drink wine
but you will never see them
intoxicated in the road.
If you follow these simple rules
you can go where you like
and be free of too many people
in one place.

We have been here before

It is the same old story of pride and glory,
the rich are moving into small romantic villages
prices are going up the poor must leave
and small shops close converted into housing
for the London mob.
It can´t be stopped the bus does not go there
any more.
New restaurants, but not for the locals
too dear, but the lucky might find a serving job.
One day the well to do will leave like the locust
the damage has been done
it takes a long time for the village to settle,
perhaps a library would help

Freedom and pandemic

Pubs and restaurant can open soon, but
schools must be shut,
beer is more alpha then education
which is not that important apart

from reading and writing, the computer
does the rest and we can rest by the bank
of idiocy while watching quiz programs
on TV.

Our ignorance suits the elite, the poor
do not strike but those with schooling do,
they ask questions, are knowledgeable
and are not impressed.

The pandemic has made authorities
more potent than they dared to hope.
For now, we do as we are told, we need
when time is right, take our freedom back.

the colour barrier

There is shooting every day in Chicago
many get killed by stray bullets shattered windows
but there are no headlines screaming
about these senseless crimes.
The gun-slingers are mostly black, and it appears
the police have given up patrolling a particular district
where the majority are dark.
we get headlines about murderous white men
and that is OK, as they fit the new narrative that
white is terrible; after all, they invaded America
and made it a powerful nation.

books

A book of vignettes, I think, is sent
too late for regrets, some of the writing has been
denied by several poetry sites
because they are rude and vulgar but right.
Not being famous I have to pay for the printing.
Like my other books, it will not sell
a single copy but wash around the internet
like pebbles on the beach, the murmur is not
sorrow but the sigh of resignation.
I have not always been like this there was a time
when I was full of romantic poetry
sent them to small magazines, before they were
eaten by the internet, and sometimes
I had a poem or two published, and it is no longer
this way, that´s OK I like writing.

Adam & Eve

If a koala bear had been sitting in the apple tree
and Eve had asked Adam to move the animal
to the appropriate tree so it could feed and sleep
there would be no need for religion and snakes
would have no poison.

It was Eve ,when she had her period, which got
the idea to cover her distress with a palm leaf,
Adam liked the design and the garment industry
was born, but it was Eve who wore and made
the first hat to protect her hair from the sun.

an Expensive item

it strange today I feel sad
I bought a new cell-phone and felt it was too expensive
I never liked spending money on myself makes
me feel guilty like do not deserves it.
I bought a suit when I was twenty a nice suit I bought
in Stockholm, it soon got too small, and I gave it
my sister husband.
Being the stinting sort, he wore it until it fell off.
When a child I never wore anything new only hand me down
I was OK with that.
The phone is black, and I feel intimidated by its sternness
when I switch it on the phone is pink and blue
looks like nursery colours to me, I have to put emails
into it and that will be a struggle.
Why did I buy this bloody phone it was an impulse
walking past a shop selling phones
the girl who sold me the phone looked beautiful
even with a face mask, I didn´t understand what she said
it is like I´m hard of hearing when I don´t see
peoples lips move.
Oh well, it is done I will wait a few days and see.

a new morning

I have a new phone the old one only rang
when feeling like it and that is not good enough
when someone takes the time calling me.
It is morning, and I read in the newspaper
the USA is upset because the no longer has free rains
in the south China sea.
When big powers talk about defence, it is not
what the mean it is about forces, perhaps with the exception
of Israel the lilliputian that wants to be big
and has partly succeeded but her feet are made of clay
she can so quickly lose it all.
The rest of the stuff was wasted ink about silly politics
and the dreaded virus that might, in the end, kill us all

a new morning

I have a new phone the old one only rang
when feeling like it and that is not good enough
when someone takes the time calling me.
It is morning, and I read in the newspaper
the USA is upset because the no longer has free rains
in the south China sea.
When big powers talk about defence, it is not
what the mean it is about forces, perhaps with the exception
of Israel the lilliputian that wants to be big
and has partly succeeded but her feet are made of clay
she can so quickly lose it all.
The rest of the stuff was wasted ink about silly politics
and the dreaded virus that might, in the end, kill us all

Morning song

it is six in the morning
I get down and move the car from
the place reserved for vans.
This the best of times cooling before the heat begins
only a few people out walking their dogs enjoying
the peace of a beginning.
I could have parked my car in the space between
two cars, but I lose my nerves, this after 60 years of driving.
In the night the wind blew hard from the sea
tiring itself out, and me too I hate the wind it takes my breath
away
leaves me a husk falling asleep in front of the TV.
Yesterday I carried water to the house, the porter usually
do this but, my wife thinks he takes too much money.
I do not agree.

Being able to carry bottles of water is better than not being
able to carry water, my heart does not agree.

The fall of communism

When free of the burden of communism
and many states became a democracies
it was a great feeling no one telling people what to do.
This and a free press became a burden for the public
who seeking order turned to the right.
When Neo- fascists came to power people rejoiced,
at last, someone to give vent to their prejudices, say,
people seeking refuge from war and most of all
the ancient hatred of the Romany people, was provided free
rein. Nothing new here people everywhere are
unpleasant hate what they do not understand,
from there to concentration camps, the road is short.

Apple tree, very pretty

The proud apple tree on top of a steep hill
and when its fruit fell, they did not stay near the trunk
but rolled down, some at a short distance and some
at the middle distance, a painter told me about,
others rolled as far as the eye could see and married
a plum tree and a new type of fruit were born.
The old tree on top of the hill bore no fruit and was
chopped down and used as winter wood, the aroma
of burning wood was wonderful.

The losing

It was a magnificent bull it dominated
and cowed any upstart bull trying to flirt with his bovines
there was a lean bull that refused to be chased off the field
it came to blows, at first it looked like the big bull
would win, but it lacked stamina, defeated it walked to the
stables the humiliation was all too much
and it refused to come out until the farmer gave it a bar
of chocolate with nuts.
The bull told itself OK, So I lost, but I´m still the biggest oxen
around this neighborhood.

Misunderstanding

the name Karen comes up often on the twitter

I took it to mean Karen Blixen, a Danish writer

who wrote about Africa in a patronizing way.

Well, it was not.

The Avenue

it is a delight to get up early, say, six o'clock
the day smells fresh and the Avenue so busy at day time
looks comely and the many commercial banks look coy
as do the hair salons, nail bars and the yoga club.
it is is a wealthy neighbourhood, my wife cuts my hair
and she goes to a modest hairdresser in a part of the town
more modest.
Why I can´t understand is why people sleep so late
get up at ten when the best part of the day is over, dormant
under skeptical duvet breathing in the stale air
of slumber that has lasted too long.
Coffee is right in the morning I get mine at the petrol station
I drink my coffee and talk to no one
and the dogs taking their owner for a stroll have stopped
barking at me wagging of tails instead.

Envy

Look at this man
he has got a Mercedes. I have not got one
my heart aches I covet this car.
No matter how hard I try, I can not afford to buy one.
But I can take this man´s pleasure in his car away.
I hate this man and his bloody car.
Scrape the bodywork on this gleaming pride, accidentally
run into him, sorry my man, the breaks failed.
Do anything to he tires of his car and put it up for sale
my glee was boundless when the vehicle was sold.
But what do you know, he bought another Mercedes.

Anatomy

Soaping in when having a shower

it struck me I have a nice rounded bum

it has three main functions

to sit on, to make me look good in jeans

and to let the undigested escape

without any hindrance.

I can not say the same about my stomach

it is to big and sags

Nothing is perfect I´m okay with that

and drink my cold beer.

Workmen

On the way to the bank this morning
four workers were shuffling shingles into big buckets
carrying the load down some steps
coming up with empty buckets filling them up again.
They had sweat on their brows; one hoped they made
enough money for the daily bread.
I may have worked long hours in my life, but not like
this lifting and carrying heavy objects, and I take it
they were poorly paid.
It seems to me people who perform hard physical
work are poorly paid in insecure work
the first to be laid off and end up sleeping in the street,
They are the people we despise
but without them the world would come to a standstill
yet we pay them a few miserable coins left in pockets

when we change our trousers.

Heatwave

It is early, but the petrol station is open
and since it is already hot, I buy two big bottles of cold water.
the heat this morning is ominous it holds no promise
of summer and fun, more like the door of hell has been left open
I hear the screams of those who are burning forever (one would
think the body would be impervious to pain)
I don´t want to go in yet sit on a cold stone bench drink water
and dream of swimming naked in the lake of love.
Of course, the lake has gone as has its tributary, the river running
from the hazy mountain.
Suddenly it hits me over the head, the voice which says,
you are 81. How the hell did you manage this?
The news isn´t helpful either saying the heatwave is no suitable

for anyone over 74.

Do they think I´m English?
I drink some cold water pretend it is from a well somewhere
hidden in my imagination of an oasis and palm trees.
I think wouldn´t it be not very good if I invented a pill that made
me

younger and younger till I disappeared unborn.

Never a mother

She was a rescued dog a tiny mite
lost in the wilderness of man and left to die.
A shivering whelp, it was a cold day
held her under my coat the trembling stopped
she fell asleep.
At the time I was rebuilding a ruin I had no
furniture only a camp bed.
I put the puppy on some canvass the workers
used when painting, and she wouldn´t hear of it
she ended up sleeping on the pillow.
A few months later, I had her spayed since I was
not sure whether staying or going back to Norway.
Thirty years later, I´m still here.
The dog, I named her Bambi,

when an adult sometimes looked mysterious,

stole from the basket of the dirty laundry building a nest behind

the sofa place by the wall.
She spent most of her time there, but after a few
days, she forgot all about it and wanted to run in the forest
chasing rabbits.
I regretted robbing her of motherhood, but my intention was good,

had I left her chances of survival would have been better not having

a litter to take care of in an unfriendly world.

his excellency

they called him excellency and a name I forgot.
As it turns out my wife´s brother was his book-keeper
a profession where the person knows a lot of secrets.
The meeting will be conducted in French.
I, thinking of Galloway calling Saddam Hussein
his excellency, must not chuckle.
Since we didn´t know what to serve him, we bought
a bottle of whiskey I had a taste and got instantly ill
the strong drink doesn´t behove me well.
She hopes he will pay for the patient´s stay with
us and the hospital bill.
I think the meeting will go well if I sit still and call
him your excellency without giggling.

Once, a princes

There was a princess
who lived in a castle on a mountain top
the princess was so delicate she had to
sleep, as in the fairy tale, on seven mattresses.
One morning when sleeping late
(she always did) she fell out of bed her mother
the queen had gone, and her father
had gone too hunting the DODO.
She was alone in the world.
Coming down from the mountain she had to
make a living, and there were jobs OK like serving food
at a cafe, but since she had been a princes
this was not possible, and her mother agreed
her daughter should not be a maid, better to starve.
In a rare moment of sanity, the princes got a job
as a security overseer that paid well enough for wine
and silk stockings.

verity

Truth is hard

bullets fly

in streets of poverty.

Gangs

pride,

getting even.

No work

no education

alcohol

drugs galore

slow suicide.

We can´t say

black

their life matters

The enemy

is the hatred

killing them

slowly.

Hard work

My uncle went to America after the war,
for an unknown reason, he didn´t like it there and came home.
But he took with him an idea he had seen, cleaning windows.
He offered to clean windows in shops it was a hard going
at first, the shopkeepers used to get a lad to do it,
but seeing a window, he did for free orders soon came in
the owner of a lingerie shop found he didn´t need
spectacles.
Soon he got the schools and became so busy he had to hire
several men to help him, he opened an office and spent
time to see the work was done correctly.
He was strict sloppy work was not tolerated he fired
people without hesitation.
When he got old, and his son showed no interest he sold
his business and went to live in Spain when he died
there was nothing for his son, the house he had bought
in Spain went to his housekeeper a hard-working woman

of fifty-two.

gods

I should have written about Zeus and other gods

how learned I would have sounded like an intellectual

and my work would have been commented on in TLS

after all people write only for those who are like them

and it is right, what do they know how a cook feels

on a ship in the middle of the Pacific ocean.

Stymied when realizing he thinks like them of course

minus the gods the Greek gods.

The are always in the background like Neptune.

The twain shall never meet,

One poet writes for the literary elite while the other for

what his mind comes up with independent of historical

figures, and himself.

A pastor and a poet

I will not compare you with a rose
it only shines a few days
while you are always blooming, said the man
coming out of the shadow of a tree.
The man was a sheep pastor, and impressed
by his words wrote it down on a flat stone, using
a smaller pointed stone as a pen.
He repeated the small poem to his wife it made
her so happy nine months later a child was born.
A poet walked past read the words, wrote them
in his notebook and published them as his own.
Poets never borrow they steal.

Black life matters

The world is in one mind,
"Black life matters."
we wholeheartedly agree with the downtrodden
and we must remedy this inequity.
With books in hands, and not guns.
To pay, like we paid the Jews for the holocaust
is to reduce suffering down to cash.
For the black race, it is about dignity and equality
nothing more nothing less.
We the working-class brown or white are slaves
under the laissez-faire economic system which
has brought poverty and death for a majority
of people: who is going to pay us?
There is only one way, change the social system
that benefit us and let us work together
to the road to racial tolerance.

Haiku

A Stygian poem

can be written in daylight

by the deadly lake.

In the lake of love

she was dead as an unsaid poem

the sun too drowned.

Seven dead nuns in a boat

had succumbed by a sea of prayers

oars dripping tears.

The racial enigma

it is a problem, are all white people responsible
for black slavery, or where they condition to think of blacks as
inferiors
because that is what the elite told them.
and since both groups of people were uneducated and stayed that way
the white worker´s only consolation was he was better for being white.
This mindset took hold to be white was better than being black but
the tragedy was the coloured believed their lower status.
The racism in the USA is endemic it will take time for the whites
to understand and value people are not by colour but by their humanity.

By the tree lines

Beautiful buildings are best seen
at a distance close up you notice flaws
and cracked concrete.

The beautiful woman at a distance
came closer, then it was morning
and she had forgotten her beauty bag

at a distance, childhood looks alluring
at a closer look, we remember tears
hunger, and poverty.

Distance makes the heart fonder and this
is a truth close up the nearness is obtrusive
we long for our private space.

Handing Trump the election

I big cities in the Us people are running wild
this is not what " black life matters" was about
a horde of people are running around destroying what is sacred
or should be, in cities of high crime.
We can argue the reason for this pointless criminality
to create mayhem for the sake of it, the fact many black people
live there and appear to gun-related gangs, not because
they are black but because they are uneducated and poor
living in squalor in drug-infested housing where only a few
survive by moving away.
The majority of letting us call them lost selfish people see
this lack of order and civility,
the high profile black leaders do little about this only come
out of their luxury home when there is a funeral
repeat the same trite words, but have nothing worthwhile to
say about crime and the woeful lack of education.
They the well off in the suburbia see this and not knowing
its origin, simply vote for Trump and so it goes on until
we live in in a failed state.

Oblique

Assassination is not a word.
I will speak out laud or glorify,
but there is the moment the word enters my mind
but I refuse to go down that road,
and in the instance I think of will make matters
worse and we might risk a military uprising.
Should we go to this forbidden place
we too become murderers even if we didn´t pull
the trigger.
This mighty man has done much harm I shudder
to think if he will grace the stage of life a long time
the implication should a bullet find its goal
and have happy people in the street celebrate
his demise by robbing jewelry shops.

The time glass

The morning takes a longer time awakening
the sun is hesitant hides in the east before showing its might.
The wind is blowing low at the entrance
it tires me out breathing becomes laborious.
I made dinner myself my wife has gone to the hospital to see
if her brother is well enough to live with us, if not we have
to send him to a place for those chronically ill.
I remember when my mother was no longer able to cope
we sent her to a home, she hated it, and in despair stopped eating.
We thought we were doing good, but we only did what was
expedient for us.
I regret this she could live longer at her own home with
with a helper coming in once a day, my mother was not that
helpless she could make her coffee in the morning
and boil an egg, it was her untidiness people reacted against
books and magazines were cluttering up the home.
She liked her self rolled cigarettes and brandy which offended
the righteous.
My sin was I should have spoken up but sided with the many
who thought what was best for her.

"after the pandemic" how often I read this
the question is, will there be an after?
If not will the last one remember to switch
off the sun.

when US industry noticed

China was a cheap place to produce their stuff
they moved the whole production to China.
This was beneficial for both, except the American workers
who as usual no one listens to when a pair of Jeans
are affordable.
Now the USA and China are squabbling like relatives
having a falling out over the right of way.
But both countries are hopelessly entwined they can´t
thrive without one another,
So, what we see is a play for the gallery not to be taken
a face value.

Cucumber

early morning
I had to eat something
found a cucumber in the fridge
that was otherwise bare.
Peeled and boiled them added a bit of butter
and a pepper
stirred well when cooked and I had
mashed cucumber.
It tasted terrific a wonder for a diabetic
I have to remember til next time
the cupboard is bare-

Corona-19 and a pigeon

Got up at eight this Sunday morning
switched on the computer and the Guardian
was full of the virus and how many had died.
I switched on the TV and watched a cartoon.
I follow the rules, wear a mask and clean
my hands, the rest is up to chance I refuse to
live in fear.
While writing these lines of homespun wisdom
a pigeon sits on the ledge if I wave my hand
it will flay away, and sometimes I wish to fly too
but I do not want to be a pigeon.

Depression

I wrote a poem that made me depressed
it took out me my natural sense of optimism
left me with the reality of the truth.
I never was a poet, only a lone man seeking
solace in an imaginary life.
Someone said my work was about my self
this is not so I write in the "I" form write
what I have read, what people have spoken and
what I think about the incredible life lived
at the outer edges of society.
Friends I had, only a few, have died
leaving me waiting for the knock on the door:
come now you can´t postpone it any longer.
I shall not go hollering into the good night,
passively submit, offer my heart and wait
for the axe to fall and I say let it be over quickly.

The future

There are moments when I wake up at night
and think of my death.
I know I will be instantly forgotten like
the great journalist Christopher Dickens
who died suddenly in Paris.
His friends will miss him but they
too will talk less about him as time goes by
I think it must be like this to be forgotten
as new people inherit the world
often for the wrong reason.
This new time frightens me although I shall
not be there and see it. My hope had been for a friendly world,

but it looks like worse is to come and I see before
a spent globe hurtling through space.

across the seas

the Pacific Ocean was like an undulating mirror
that day the ship was on its way to Nagasaki
which for the young crew onboard meant nothing
it is incredible how quickly a war is forgotten.
Under the ocean, there were hundreds of sunken ships
there must have been much suffering and deaths
and many books were written on how successful America
had been beating the enemy into submission.
Nagasaki was like building site the Phoenix was rising
up from the ashes shinier than before.
I came across a neglected Portuguese Cemetery of mostly
young men who had succumbed to pestilence long
before Japan became a modern state
the only visible place that told of deaths the rest was
face masks because of building dust and beer.
I looked at the faces in the street this was not an oppressed
people, the war was behind them they looked at the future.

the high Jump

Over the bay I saw a rainbow dripping colors

into the turquoise water.

Nothing can be that beautiful I have seen it all

Jumped from the balcony but the terrace underneath

ours was bigger.

Nothing was broken the flat was empty except

for a Picasso painting and one by a man called Larsen,

concluded the people who lived there were Norwegian

I walked up the steps to my flat, let myself in

the rainbow was gone, but on the surface of the water

I saw spilled diesel oil that often has a rainbow

color but lacks beauty.

where have you been, she said.

nowhere really just jumping about a bit.

The Soviet Union has gone.

I was in the Soviet Union once
through the Dardanelles into the Black sea
to an oil town.
We walked ashore the was a big avenue
empty of cars side roads were dark
and everywhere a picture of Stalin he
was around in case we should forget.
It was a drab place and appeared as it was in deep mourning.
We found a restaurant, white table cloth and Stalin.
The men wore suits made by a tailor who used to make
uniform. But the suits were too much suit.
I drank white wine and thought it was lovely, unsteadily we
walked back on board.
Some of the crew had bought Caviar which the later
sold in Sweden. I like fried cod roe, well we can´t all
be refined.
Why do they make people's life so dreary I noticed
the same in East Germany, it is like they want people
to go to bed at eight.
all this has changed neon light and bars open to twelve
nightclubs too although I have never been in any night club
this has to do with my frugality,
why should I buy expensive beer when I can get cheap
lager just around the corner.

Am I a snob

Going for lunch at the downstairs restaurant
the staff was busy and had no time to greet us
the food we had ordered beforehand arrive an hour late
I had a glass of wine but only took one sip put the wine aside
my irritation was palpable, and I wouldn't say I like being ignored.
This happens when you visit a restaurant too often.
the food, when it served was good but complained about the wine
I was offered another glass but declined.
Made note not to go there for sometimes.
At the building's reception, the new porter did´t bother to get up
he was dressed in a T-shirt and wore jeans continued to read his
newspaper,

his presence cheapened the building which has a splendid name.
I dislike rude people, the lack of manners I sometimes encounter.
Please and Thank you, are not swear words.
I read a bit fell asleep when waking up I thought never mind
they can go and fuck off.

Modern democracy

Think of an egg hollow it out drink its albumen and yolk
the empty shell cracks easily and we call it democracy
and free expression which is subjected to unwritten laws.
You can call Trump a son of the devil, but not wish him
hanged, like Mussolini, was hung.

You will be subject to a sensor and put in a cell for a night,
democracy is a schoolyard with high walls if rules
are following the power to be will smile benightedly, you are
a useful idiot and they shower you will see the illusion
of richness if you play their game.

The world is now a fascist state, and they spy on you in shops
or in the street and what you say on the phone is recorded
because if you think and turn they will lose credibility,
followed by a revolution that will set you free providing
they do not infiltrate and snatch your power base away.

Helge, my Brother

My brother Helge died suddenly
I feel devastated although we had the same father
family affairs kept us apart
I feel the loss of Helge sincerely like the last anchor chain
is broken and I drift alone on the endless ocean.
Helge was much younger than me, 52 years old and
I feel he got a raw deal, and his health was never good yet
he should have lived longer, but destiny has its own will.
I miss him profoundly and regret I did´t get to know
him better.
So goodbye brother till we see each other again.

the man they did not hang

It appears Donald Trump has

monopolized the Facebook he uses it

as a propaganda tool

I overlook his rants and hope other

Facebook readers do the same.

Unfortunately many of his base also

read the Facebook and the still chose

to believe him and that is their prerogative.

One remembers the Nazi regime the people

believed the lies to their country was

ruined and humiliated.

The alternative to Trump is the motley

Joe Biden whose politics is firmly planted in

big business he will avoid taxing them.

Still we hope he wins the election

because of his running mate Carmela Harris

who might charm the old man to

be benevolent towards the working class,

small farms, but not the Agro-business.

Getting old

Reading the papers this morning
was a sad affair, so many of the famous stars of yesteryear
had succumbed to old age.

They were as I´m in their eighties and I felt their death
as a sting in my heart, soon it will be my time to go
I accept this, but will not sink into depression.

Of everything that has happened in my life I feel no guilt
hindsight is a waste of time, my lack of success is a bonus
I have no laurel to rest on and can do as I please.

What is noticeable is my lack of understanding
of a language that has changed it is more lose now and
that is good, but it takes some effort.

The river of words I bathed in, flows slower now it is
a struggle to find the right expression, I feel as I´m
learning to swim in colder water.

Living in Portugal as I do is fine they are gentler here
and has patience when I struggle for words in shops
I have to resort to poetic expressions.

They smile broadly and think what a funny old man
I don´t mind, my wife leans heavily on her crutch,

and she gets first in line. We try to look decrepit.

At the end of this month, I need a new driving license
I have spring in my steps, luckily my eyesight is good
and the heart and diabetes go unmentioned.

The lady who cleans the dead

The woman who washed and dressed
the dead body of my wife´s brother
came for a visit (getting paid)
I noticed the nails of her hands were manicured gray
did she in her daily work meet more dead bodies
than live ones.
She looked beach clean, bet she used gloves when
eating lunch.
She looked ill at ease, this because I sat there gaping
studying her like she was an alien,
She was deeply tanned this was understandable
spending so much time in a cellar full of corpses.
Why had she chosen this profession, perhaps she
had studied to be a doctor and failed.
A new idea struck me if I suddenly died, she would
perhaps. Wash me, put lipstick on my dead lips
and rouge on my cheeks.
I smiled broadly at her nodded to what she said
showed my best side, you never know.

the gay-friend

There was an old hotel near where I walked home it had a little bar
that closed early I went in for a beer, the barman did not see me at first
not that I am a student of people. but I have observed life, and I thought

this man was gay
I had a beer and to my surprise found him erudite with a sharp wit that
matches my own I had in the desert of "Englishness" saw a man I could
converse with, we agreed to meet at a bar further up the road when
he closed.
He came sat down and said: before anyone tells you I´m gay, after
a pause
I said I know OK he was a jobbing actor and when "resting" took
any work
that came along.
We met twice a week for lunch he told stories from the world of
acting and
I told tales from the sea, but most of all we laughed at the crazy world
When he met the man who became his boyfriend I didn´t see him so often
but we still had lunch once a month if that.
I didn´t see him for a while assumed he had found an acting job, but
I was told he had died after cancer surgery about a month ago.
and that was that

Home from the sea

he is walking into the town,
new trousers and jacket
bought in America, shiny shoes.
He smiles to the girls who smile back
he has money
in his pocket home from the sea.
He has many friends
they come in the bar to say halo,
beer is flowing he pays
home from the sea flush of money.
Smells of expensive after-shave
bought in America.
He is walking into town,
his jacket is no longer new and shoes
not shiny
he is broke does not go to the bar.
It is a dull day.
He goes down to the office
that hires seamen, ask if there is a job.
Not today, come back tomorrow.
The way back home is long and
rain falls.

America

I used to love America we never said the USA
as a young seaman, it was the place to buy T. shirts, jeans
and white I never forget the name, Arrow shirts
the people full of optimism everything was possible
and the workers were relatively affluent.
the racial aspect never bothered us; we saw black workers
and white workers toiling on the harbour.
I was reading much back then and discovered I had lived
in a bubble.
In New Orleans, I came face to face with racism I hat
met an enormous black foreman he invited me to
the town centre the restaurant I liked he said we could
not go into, you see, they don´t want people of my colour.
OK, we went to a lesser place had a splendid meal
listened to jazz music.
He insisted following me to the ship, and I remember some
white shouting nigger lover. Onboard iI read a novel by
James Baldwin, I didn´t sleep that night
Years later coming back to the USA, it had changed was
a more challenging place and there was on the radio,
endless talk
about the peril of socialism and the need to go to war.
I was older now and self- educated, knew it was no point
arguing with people who had been brainwashed.

Flapping wings

The extinct bird of evil

survived in the mindset of many,

Flapping its wings

casting dark shadows

of things to come.

Trump, I hear you say,

the show starter

his antics merely funny.

The darkness begins to fall

in Europe

turning back like the salmon

to its origin.

Nazism is on the rise again

you hear its demand

from north to south,

your hear from democratic

politicians

changing hymn sheet.

Too much freedom is painful

for the people who think

they have the right to speak freely.

Order is the word we hear

we must restore order.

Our liberty is a stake

we must wake up against consumerism

and don´t be led astray

rise up against Nazism now

tomorrow it is too late.

The war of decency

There was a time when showing
toes in public were regarded as a sexual crime
men wore boots and thick socks.
Women wore lighter footwear but covered
up to the ankles.
Some perverts sat in parks shocking passing
women waving their toes, not forget females
of ill repute showing an ankle.
time was changing they always do, sandals
came in the church was against it but was
unable to stop this tide of modernity.
it was legal to wear sandals with woolly socks
for men and black nylon socks for women,
Many young females wore socks so tight
they hinted of toes underneath.
The clerics became middle-class and liberal
everything was OK; God was all-forgiving.

We kill children

They die in Yemen so small they are
the dead children, some look like rag dolls
smeared with blood drying in the sun.
Some have no arms or legs their school had been bombed
our manufactured bombs which we say are only sold
to a friendly nation.
A friendly country does not need bombs, the very notion
is contempt.
I remember a song, "Who are you kidding, mister Hitler."
Children starving to death they have no food-banks
in Yemen, and as we know it is always the poorest
who have nowhere to hide.
The very rich have built bunkers to ride out the nuclear war the
surely will come,

but will it be
a world worth living in for their children.
Every hour a child dies in Yemen. It doesn't make headlines
anymore.
Yemen is sinking into the morass like Libya that
is no longer a state but a hideout for people who sell children into
slavery and paedophilia.
Every hour a child dies in Yemen...

he sacred leader

who is this self- appointed honourable professor
who likes to dress up in uniforms and send pictures of himself
talking about Jesus Christ in glowing terms.
elegant and with appeared as expensive rings he strikes
up an attitude of a cult leader.
he is also an ambassador of soulful poetry and has vowed
to regal us with eight verses in eight days
I understand he was a former sergeant in the US military
hence his fondness of wearing self- made uniforms.
I´m sceptical religious beliefs is displayed this way given
out diplomas to all and sundry.
Is he a fraud, a snake-oil salesman who knows how important
it is for the second rate to be reckoned and give them
a sense of being famous.
I remember this man when he wrote modest poems that
as poems do drown in the mass of inconsequential poems
churned out on a daily bases.
as it is I would hope he will refrain from his organized religion
on my page.

September storm

There was a storm last night hitting the wall
of my bedroom howling with anger and ill will
no sleep for the wicked.
Got up at six put on pyjamas and a T. shirt
(like to sleep naked) I say this just in case
you like to come for a visit.
At in my study, the wind sensed this and changed direction
banging and rattling the window demented with fury.
I retreated to the kitchen
had a coffee fell asleep watching morning TV

end of human life has begun

Birds of all size and variety
are falling from the sky
the migration got too hot for them
tired wings cannot fly
the only animal that appears to thrive
is the crocodile
In Australia and attack lone walkers.
Trees too migrate seeking a cooler
and wetter clime in the north/west
and since they cannot walk
send an advanced army of leaves
to begin a new forest.
we are doomed, but is in denial
of a summer when pandemic kept
us indoors

The Illusion

I met a group of people I vaguely thought familiar
after a while it came to me and said, you are
the same people I met 15 years ago, glad laughter
we wondered if you had forgotten us.
I was baffled an old dream had produced a new one
or was there no past it all happens now.
Or did our lives had two levels one that is conscious
has a sunrise, and one we only see by accident like
someone had forgotten to lock the door.
Got up from the table and bid farewell, have to go
take the train to the valley where I once was a cobbler
and I only made wooden clogs with leather uppers.
Sitting on the bed, I could not make up my mind what
was a dream or the truth, when daylight came I knew
that dreams too were truths

Wherefore

there are a question philosophers and goat herders
has in common with the rest of us the modest multitude
the query is, what is the purpose of our life
from a single sperm cell to fighting it way survival and life
and we ask for what purpose?
we know the outer shell of what we are is based on
the environment we live in, such as education. friends
we meet and dream.
but the question remains, why are we survivors and what
is the purpose of life that often changes unplanned by us.
The cynical among us have an easy answer,
but they cannot tell you why they become suspicious and
why Adolf became Hitler.
The nearest answer I can think of that life is a prelude
to a new existence an astral life form free of ego, and ownership
will not be asked, we are free truly
liberated of the life that weighed us down on earth.
God is not in this picture, an abstraction we give thanks to when a
war ends
and pray to during a new war which is like wildfire
there are always conflicts that are not planned but just happen
on life on our planet.
humanity is like a lost child in an amusement park, the colours
of the blinking light are a warning, and outside the park it is dark
we look for guidance but cannot find the answer.

Wherefore

there are a question philosophers and goat herders
has in common with the rest of us the modest multitude
the query is, what is the purpose of our life
from a single sperm cell to fighting it way survival and life
and we ask for what purpose?
we know the outer shell of what we are is based on
the environment we live in, such as education. friends
we meet and dream.
but the question remains, why are we survivors and what
is the purpose of life that often changes unplanned by us.
The cynical among us have an easy answer,
but they cannot tell you why they become suspicious and
why Adolf became Hitler.
The nearest answer I can think of that life is a prelude
to a new existence an astral life form free of ego, and ownership
will not be asked, we are free truly
liberated of the life that weighed us down on earth.
God is not in this picture, an abstraction we give thanks to when a
war ends
and pray to during a new war which is like wildfire
there are always conflicts that are not planned but just happen
on life on our planet.
humanity is like a lost child in an amusement park, the colours
of the blinking light are a warning, and outside the park it is dark
we look for guidance but cannot find the answer.

tabula rasa

when we are born a child has no memory
one can say clean slates, after a few days they pick up
the basic like crying when hungry
from there on we fill the baby with what we know
a knowledge handed down from our parents, and the child
when it learns to read believes without reflection
what they are told must be the truth.
sometimes the child has a new thought, and it says what if this
is not valid, that is when the memory it didn´t have
is remembered, something that is clean and true about the life
we live an illusion made up of a generation of lies told
to keep us docile, most children dismiss this idea and go on
playing football, but a few listen to the voice of verity
and not knowing how to shut up tell everyone that life is more
then they have ever imagined.
those children are embarking on a long track that sometimes
leads to jail terms and sometimes to an early death
by those who know they are speaking the truth but try to say
the child has a criminal mind.
the road ahead of the few are long, and there is no happy ending
except the knowledge they have gives them comfort

People I meet on and off the screen

I like to watch a TV program, Father Brown
the actors are like old friends I know what they are thinking
one of the most charming figures is the police inspector
he naturally gets everything wrong from the start
and is very rude to Father Brown.
Of course, I see them as actors in real life they are totally
different if I meet one of them in the street
I would have said, look at him he seems like an actor
I have seen on TV and walked on.
I once met Cliff Richards in a paper shop he was buying
the Telegraph (a rightwing paper)
He was a small man and pleased that I didn't fawn all
over him. We had lunch together, at a little place that had
few tourists, and with some wine, he was good company
relaxed too away from the fans.
When in Algarve I met many actors and found them
to be kind and thoughtful people, and not the way the often
are portrait in the "Sun" and other shitty papers.

Drugs

I never showed my dogs any tricks that appear to please
people she grew a puppy to an adult, mind I sometimes
patted her and she had the habit of using my feet as a pillow
when I was watching TV. when she got older, she got a bit
grumpy when I moved my feet.
Today I watched how they killed Pablo Escobar, a drug trader
a murderous gangster, all his costumers, live in the USA.
As usual in this cases, someone else took over and it will
continue and this how capitalism work.
there is a hallowed family selling opium in large scale they
by bribing doctors to push this wonder medicine that
that made people addicted, well opium is addictive whatever
name you to put on the label.
this family still flogs their wonder pills I will not use the name
but they have killed more people than Escobar.

Glorious Sweden

When the virus struck the virologist
put their faith in herd immunity six thousand
people died mostly those over sixty which
is a high number for a small country.
Sweden has been able to stabilize the number
of affected people but the virus is still there
regrouping ready to strike again,
This time it will target the younger generation
will fall victim of this deadly disease now
when winter comes, and nightclubs are
an alluring placc.
The virologists have failed to see this virus
is not your common flu, that also is here to stay,
but we have a vaccine for this.
Now that all the elderly are dead we can say
Sweden is a young country but, alas, not a better one.
What do I know, perhaps this was intentional.

waiting in a line

In front of the multi-bank window
an older man was transferring money, and like me he got
confused by all the numbers and had to do it again.
I was patient thought of loftier things is hell coal-fired
or do they use electrical energy for the doomed ones?
How is it possible to burn forever without actually burning
and turning into ashes the flames are like a cosy blanket
on a sofa near the oven.
lost in reveries, I didn´t notice the man had gone
a woman who was behind me took his place she had in
her plastic bag sanitary bin this I presumed was because
she was middle-aged and leaky.
she also had a loaf of bread and two tins of sardines food that
was of no interest, she had no right to take my place.

the tapered

It started with great ambition six lanes motorway
after some time it narrowed and became a 4 line.
That didn´t last it got narrower two lines will do.
then on the road with a line in the middle and that was
OK as well til the asphalt disappeared driving on grit
causes many punctures.
A track, get off an walk to reach the blue mountain-
when getting there, it was slippery and cold.
There must be another mountain that fits the dream.
The highway was optimist youth pointing out stars
not seeing the road got narrower, and it was too late.
The trail is for old men who wait for a miracle or
for someone telling them where to go when the path
leads them to nowhere in particular while dreaming
of dancing nymphs in the glade.

Fishery

He is a fisherman from Guiana
doesn´t do Tonga, but the sea is blue.
His face is a map of America.
He fishes sharks (not Hemingway)
one of them took his arm.
Vengeance is mine, said the lord.
Crap !!! He says
and set red sail for China.

Arguments

The captain of our ship
and the chief officer was not best of friends,
one day when the chief had imbibed a few whiskeys
the captain wrote in the logbook,
today the chief officer is drunk.
Infuriated the chief in the same logbook wrote,
today the captain is sober.